Wetlands of the Boston Harbor Islands National Recreation Area

by

Ralph W. Tiner, John Q. Swords, and Herbert C. Bergquist

U.S. Fish & Wildlife Service
National Wetlands Inventory Program
Northeast Region
300 Westgate Center Drive
Hadley, MA 01035

Prepared for the U.S. Department of Interior, National Park Service

February 2003

Table of Contents

Appendices

A: Legend for wetland and deepwater habitat classification following Cowardin et al. 1979.

B: Extent of wetlands and deepwater habitats in and around the Boston Harbor Islands NRA based on an update of seven NWI maps in this locale.

Introduction

The National Park Service (NPS) needs current information on the distribution and types of wetlands occurring within the Boston Harbor Islands National Recreation Area (Boston Harbor Islands NRA) to aid its efforts to improve management of Park resources. Such information includes maps and digital data for computer analysis using Geographic Information System (GIS) technology.

The U.S. Fish and Wildlife Service (FWS) is mapping wetlands across the country as part of its National Wetlands Inventory (NWI) Program. The NWI employs aerial photointerpretation techniques to identify, delineate, and classify wetlands on aerial photography (see website at: http://wetlands.fws.gov). NWI products include large-scale maps (1:24,000/1:25,000) and accompanying digital data. The NWI has prepared wetland maps for numerous Federal and state agencies, including the NPS.

Given the national scope of the NWI, mid- to high-altitude aerial photography (1:40,000 and smaller) is typically used for wetland mapping. At the outset of the NWI in the late 1970s, 1:80,000 black and white aerial photography was used. This quad-centered photography was acquired by the U.S. Geological Survey (USGS) to produce updates of large-scale topographic maps and orthophotoquads in some areas. With this imagery, the NWI mapped wetlands 3-5 acres and larger. In the 1980s, this photography was replaced by 1:58,000 color infrared photography derived the USGS's National High-Altitude Aerial Photography Program. The NWI used this photography to map wetlands 1-3 acres in size or more. In the late 1980s, the USGS began acquiring 1:40,000 color infrared and/or black and white aerial photography through its National Aerial Photography Program. With this imagery, NWI's target mapping unit was about one acre in size or more. Tiner (1990, 1999) described limitations of aerial photography for wetland mapping.

For the Boston Harbor area, the original NWI maps were produced over 20 years ago based on late 1970s 1:80,000 aerial photography. These maps were updated about ten years ago with mid-1980s 1:58,000 photography (the most recent photography available at that time). The most current mid-altitude aerial photography available for this area is 1995 1:40,000 color infrared photography.

In 2001, the National Park Service provided funds to the FWS to do the following:

- Update NWI maps and digital data for the Boston Harbor Islands NRA
- Enhance the digital database to include hydrogeomorphic-type descriptors for landscape position, landform, and water flow path
- Prepare a wetlands inventory report for the Boston Harbor Islands NRA
- Produce a color-coded map showing the wetlands by type within the Boston Harbor Islands NRA

This work would provide the NPS with needed wetland information for resource planning and management.

The purpose of this report is to summarize the results of this effort, with emphasis on the wetlands associated with the islands in the designated Boston Harbor Islands NRA. Generalized wetland maps are included in this publication. More detailed map information can be obtained from the NWI website (http://wetlands.fws.gov) where NWI digital map data can be downloaded for GIS applications or data can be directly viewed through the "interactive mapper tool."

Study Area

The Boston Harbor Islands NRA is located within Boston Harbor and neighboring bays (Dorchester, Quincy, and Hingham) in eastern Massachusetts. It contains 34 islands: Bumpkin, Button, Calf, Deer, Gallops, Georges, Grape, Great Brewster, Green, Hangman, Langlee, Little Brewster, Little Calf, Long, Lovells, Middle Brewster, Moon, Nixes Mate, Nut, Outer Brewster, Peddocks, Raccoon, Ragged, Rainsford, Sarah, Shag Rocks, Sheep, Slate, Snake, Spectacle, The Graves, Thompson, Webb Memorial, and Worlds End (Figure 1).

Figure 1. Location of Boston Harbor Islands National Recreation Area, with major islands highlighted.

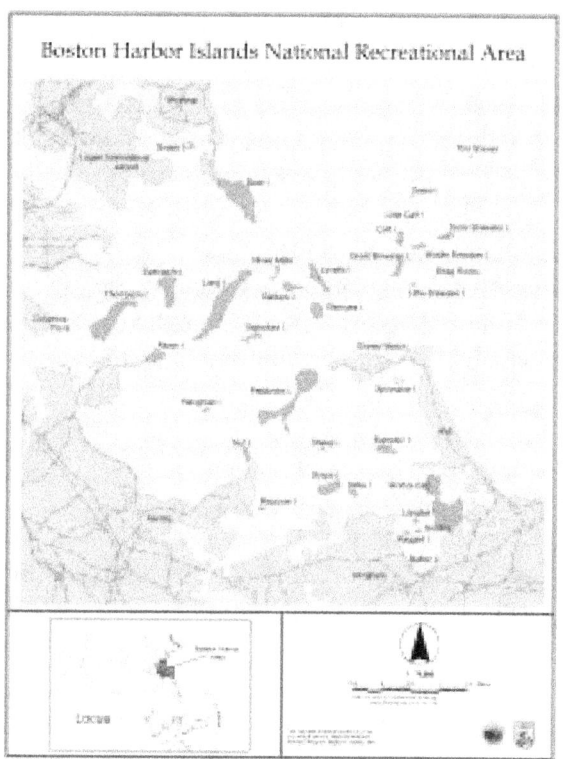

(Click here for image)

Methods

The FWS used conventional photointerpretation techniques to identify and classify wetlands and deepwater habitats in the Boston Harbor Islands NRA.[1] Color infrared, mid-altitude aerial photography (1:40,000) acquired in 1995 was used for this project. Wetlands were initially classified according to the FWS's "Classification of Wetlands and Deepwater Habitats of the United States" (Cowardin et al. 1979) – the federal data standard established by the Federal Geographic Data Committee. Figure 2 shows the boundary between the marine and estuarine systems - the dominant ecosystems of the Boston Harbor Islands NRA. Baseline digital wetland data for this inventory came from the NWI wetland database derived from 1980s-era aerial photographs. These data were revised through interpretation of the 1995 aerial photography. Photointerpretation was performed on a digital transfer scope that permitted simultaneous viewing of aerial photos and existing digital data. Edits were made directly to the digital database. Collateral data sources used during this updated inventory included data on intertidal wetlands compiled by Rich Bell of the New England Aquarium (results now published in Bell et al. 2002), NWI maps/digital data, eelgrass distribution data from the State's geographic information system (MassGIS at: http://www.state.ma.us/mgis), and U.S. Geological Survey topographic maps and accompanying digital raster graphics and digital line graphs for hydrology (e.g., rivers, streams, lakes, and ponds). Computer-generated maps were produced and statistics on wetland acreages were tabulated using Arcview 3.1 GIS software.

A field trip was conducted in the study area on October 23, 2001. Visits were made to the following islands: Thompson, Peddocks, and Grape.

After revising the wetlands digital data, hydrogeomorphic-type attributes were added to the database to provide a more complete characterization of each wetland and deepwater habitat. These attributes included descriptors for landscape position (the relationship between a wetland and a waterbody), landform (the physical shape of a wetland), water flow path (the directional flow of surface water), and waterbody types following Tiner (2000). The addition of these attributes allowed the FWS to perform a preliminary assessment of wetland functions for the Boston Harbor Islands NRA. The following functions were evaluated: surface water detention, nutrient transformation, sediment retention, coastal storm surge detention and shoreline stabilization, fish and shellfish habitat, waterfowl and waterbird habitat, and other wildlife habitat.[2] Table 1 summarizes the correlations between functions and various wetland types for Northeast wetlands. Note that since the study area is characterized by relatively small islands surrounded by marine and estuarine waters, most of wetland types listed in Table 1 are not present. The rationale for these correlations is reported elsewhere (e.g., Tiner et al. 1999, 2000).

---

[1] The intertidal zone around most islands was relatively discrete, except for three islands (Button, Sarah, and Ragged) in Hingham Harbor that were connected with tidal flats extending to the mainland; a 75m boundary was placed around them for calculating wetland acreage associated with these islands.

[2] Given the lack of perennial streams on the islands, one function listed in Table 1 - streamflow maintenance - was not evaluated.

Figure 2. Boundary between the marine and estuarine systems in the Boston Harbor Islands NRA.

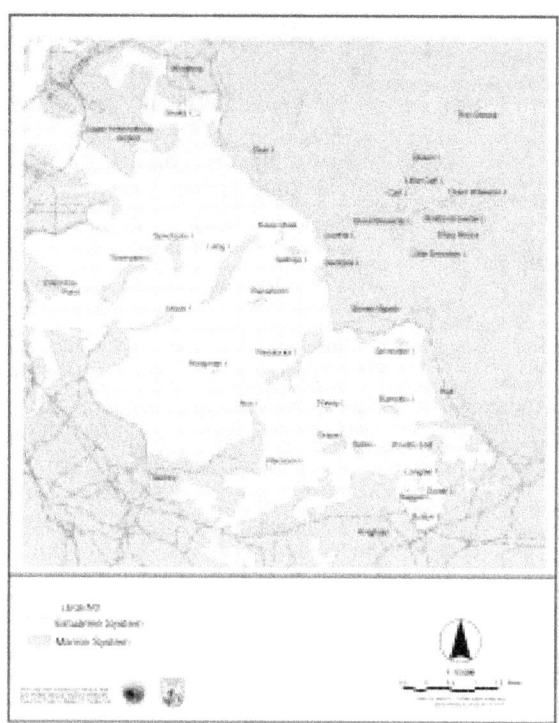

(Click here for image)

5

Table 1. Correlations between wetland functions and types for Northeast wetlands. An asterisk (*) indicates a wetland type restricted to coastal waters. <u>Note</u>: Most of the wetland types do not occur in the Boston Harbor Islands NRA, since it is comprised on relatively small islands. See an NWI map legend for coding (Appendix A).

Function	Predicted Level of Significance	Wetland Types
Surface Water Detention	High	Estuarine Fringe*, Estuarine Basin*, Estuarine Island*, Lentic Basin, Lentic Fringe, Lentic Flat associated with reservoirs and flood control dams, Lotic Basin, Lotic Floodplain, Lotic Fringe, Lotic Island associated with Floodplain region, Lotic Island basin, Marine Fringe*, Marine Island*, Ponds Throughflow (in-stream) and associated Fringe and Basin wetlands, Ponds Bidirectional and associated wetlands, Ponds Bidirectional Tidal and associated wetlands*, Terrene Throughflow Basin
	Moderate	Lotic Flat, Lotic Island flat, Terrene Interfluve, Other Terrene Basins, Other Ponds and associated wetlands
Streamflow Maintenance	High	Headwater Wetlands (Terrene, Lotic, and Lentic), Headwater Ponds and Lakes (classified as PUB...on NWI)
	Moderate	Lotic (Nontidal) Floodplain, Throughflow Ponds and Lakes (classified as PUB on NWI) and their associated wetlands, Terrene Outflow wetlands (associated with streams not major rivers), Outflow Ponds and Lakes (classified as PUB... on NWI), "Natural" Throughflow Ponds and Lakes (classified as PUB...on NWI)
Nutrient Transformation	High	Vegetated wetlands with C, E, F, and H water regimes, Mixed unconsolidated bottom-vegetated wetlands with C, E, F, and H water regimes (this includes Lotic, Terrene, and Lentic wetlands - mostly floodplain, basin, interfluve-basin, and fringe types), Vegetated tidal wetlands (and mixes with nonvegetated classes) with N, P, R, and T water regimes*
	Moderate	Vegetated wetlands with A water regime, Lotic tidal vegetated wetlands with S water regime*
Retention of Sediments	High	Estuarine Basin*, Estuarine Fringe (excluding rocky shore)*, Estuarine Island (excluding rocky shore)*, Lentic Basin, Lentic Fringe (vegetated only), Lentic Island (vegetated), Lotic Basin, Lotic Floodplain,Lotic Fringe (vegetated only), Lotic Island, Throughflow Pond (in-stream) and associated vegetated wetlands, Bidirectional Ponds and associated wetlands, Bidirectional Tidal Ponds and associated wetlands*, Terrene Throughflow Basin
	Moderate	Lotic Flat, Lotic Tidal Fringe nonvegetated)*, Marine Fringe (excluding rocky shore)*, Marine Island (excluding rocky shore)*, Other Terrene Basins, Terrene Interfluve Basin, Terrene wetlands associated with ponds, Other Ponds and associated wetlands (excluding slope wetlands)

Table 1 (continued).

Function	Predicted Level of Significance	Wetland Types
Coastal Storm Surge Detention and Shoreline Stabilization	High	Estuarine Basin*, Estuarine Fringe*, Lotic Tidal Fringe*, Marine Fringe*
Provision of Fish and Shellfish Habitat	High	Estuarine Emergent wetland* (including mixtures with other types), Estuarine Unconsolidated Shore*, Estuarine Intertidal Reef*, Estuarine Aquatic Bed*, Estuarine Intertidal Rocky Shore*, Lacustrine Semipermanently Flooded (excluding wetlands along intermittent streams), Lacustrine Littoral Aquatic Bed, Lacustrine Littoral Unconsolidated Bottom/Vegetated wetland, Lacustrine Littoral Vegetated wetland with a Permanently Flooded water regime, Marine Aquatic Bed*, Marine Intertidal Rocky Shore*, Marine Intertidal Unconsolidated Shore*, Marine Intertidal Reef*, Palustrine Semipermanently Flooded (excluding wetlands along intermittent streams; must be associated with a *permanent* waterbody such as PUBH, L1UBH, or R2/R3UBH), Palustrine Aquatic Bed, Palustrine Unconsolidated Bottom/Vegetated wetland, Palustrine Vegetated wetland with a Permanently Flooded water regime, Palustrine Tidal Emergent wetlands with N, R, or T water regimes (excluding "R" wetlands where EM5 is only dominant)*, Ponds (PUBH.. on NWI; not PUBF) associated with Semipermanently Flooded vegetated wetlands, Riverine Tidal Emergent wetland*, Riverine Tidal Unconsolidated Shore wetlands (excluding those with an "S" water regime)*
	Moderate	Lentic wetlands that are PEM1E, Lotic River or Stream wetlands that are PEM1E (including mixtures with Scrub-Shrub or Forested wetlands), Semipermanently flooded Phragmites wetlands (PEM5F) where associated with a permanent waterbody, Other Ponds and associated Fringe wetlands (i.e., Terrene Fringe-pond) (excluding industrial, stormwater treatment/detention, and similar ponds in highly disturbed landscapes)
	Important for Stream Shading	Lotic Stream wetlands that are Palustrine Forested wetlands (includes mixes where forested wetland predominates; excluding those along intermittent streams) (*Note that although forested wetlands are designated as important for stream shading, forested uplands provide similar functions*)

Table 1 (continued).

Function	Predicted Level of Significance	Wetland Types
Provision of Waterfowl and Waterbird Habitat	High	Estuarine Aquatic Bed*, Estuarine Emergent wetlands*, Estuarine Unconsolidated Shore* (except S water regime), Estuarine Intertidal Reef*, Lacustrine Semipermanently Flooded, Lacustrine Littoral Aquatic Bed, Lacustrine Littoral Vegetated wetlands with an H water regime, Lacustrine Unconsolidated Shores (F, E, or C water regimes; mudflats), Marine Aquatic Bed*, Marine Intertidal Reef*, Marine Unconsolidated Shore*, Palustrine Semipermanently Flooded (excluding PEM5F, but including mixtures containing EM5), Palustrine Aquatic Bed, Palustrine Vegetated wetlands with an H water regime, Palustrine Unconsolidated Shores (F, E, or C water regimes; mudflats), Seasonally Flooded/Saturated Palustrine wetlands impounded or beaver-influenced (all vegetation types [except PEM5Eh and PEM5Eb] and associated PUB waters, Palustrine Unconsolidated Shores (F, E, and C water regimes; mudflats), Lotic River or Stream wetlands that are PEM1E (including mixtures with Scrub-Shrub or Forested wetlands; excluding PEM5E), Ponds associated with Semipermanently Flooded Vegetated wetlands, Palustrine Tidal Emergent wetlands (PEM1R and PEM1T and mixes with other EM and with SS and FO; excluding wetlands where EM5 is the only EM), Riverine Tidal Emergent wetlands, Riverine Tidal Unconsolidated Shores (except with S water regime)
	Moderate	Phragmites wetlands that are Seasonally Flooded/Saturated and wetter (PEM5E; PEM5F; PEM5H, and PEM5R) *and* associated with a waterbody, Other Lacustrine Littoral Unconsolidated Bottom, Other Palustrine Unconsolidated Bottom (excluding industrial, commercial, stormwater detention, wastewater treatment, and similar ponds), Palustrine Emergent wetlands (including mixtures with Scrub-shrub) that are Seasonally Flooded and associated with permanently flooded waterbodies
	Significant for Wood Duck	Lotic wetlands (excluding those along intermittent streams) that are Forested or Scrub-shrub or mixtures of these types, Lotic wetlands that are mixed Forested/Emergent or Unconsolidated Bottom/Forested with a E, F, or R water regime
Provision of Other Wildlife Habitat	High	Large vegetated wetlands (≥20 acres, excluding open water and nonvegetated areas), small diverse wetlands (10-20 acres with 2 or more covertypes; excluding EM5 as one of the covertypes), areas with large numbers of small isolated wetlands (within an upland forest matrix), interconnected wetlands (with corridor vegetation mostly intact)
	Moderate	Other vegetated wetlands (including Phragmites wetlands but excluding aquatic beds)

Results

Digital Inventory Data

Digital data for seven NWI maps were updated as part of this project: 1) East Half of Boston North, 2) West Half of Lynn, 3) East Half of Boston South, 4) West Half of Hull, 5) East Half of Hull, 6) West Half of Weymouth, and 7) East Half of Weymouth. Standard NWI digital data (i.e., Cowardin et al. classifications) for these quads are posted on the NWI website at: http://wetlands.fws.gov. Enhanced digital NWI data including attributes for describing wetlands by landscape position, landform, and water flow path and waterbodies by additional properties have been forwarded to the National Park Service for inclusion in the Boston Harbor Islands NRA database. In the future, such data will likely be added to geospatial data posted on the NWI website.

Wetland Status in the Boston Harbor Islands NRA

A total of 1,276 acres of wetlands were inventoried in the Boston Harbor Islands NRA (Table 2; Figure 3). The estuarine and marine systems dominated this area (Figure 2). Consequently, most (or 76%) of the wetlands were estuarine types, with marine wetlands making up most of the remainder (22%). Only two percent of the wetlands were freshwater types (palustrine wetlands).

Tidal flats (estuarine and marine unconsolidated shore wetlands) predominated. They covered 873 acres of intertidal habitat and represented 68 percent of the wetlands. Reefs formed by blue mussel (Mytilus edulis) and intertidal rocky shores were present in equal amounts, with 87 and 83 acres, respectively. Nearly 82 acres of estuarine emergent wetland (i.e., salt/brackish marsh) were inventoried. Only 31 acres of palustrine wetlands were mapped and 75 percent was represented by freshwater ponds (palustrine unconsolidated bottom and shore). Vegetated wetlands accounted for only 7.7 acres or 25 percent of the palustrine wetlands.

Wetlands were most abundant in association with six islands (Table 3). Four islands had nearly 100 or more acres: Thompson Island (211 acres), Peddocks (118), Long (116) and Worlds End (99).

The extent of wetlands classified by hydrogeomorphic descriptors (i.e., landscape position, landform, and water flow path) is summarized in Table 4 and illustrated in Figure 4. Of the estuarine wetlands, nearly all were fringe types located along the margins of the islands. Only 12.4 acres of estuarine wetlands were classified as islands. These island wetlands were tidal flats that are exposed at low tide. Nearly 15 acres of intertidal rocky islands were inventoried in the marine system, while most marine wetlands fringed upland islands. Almost 31 acres of freshwater wetlands (including ponds) were associated with the Boston Harbor islands; most were isolated ponds.

While the islands are surrounded by marine and estuarine waters, deepwater habitats were scarce on the islands themselves. Only 4.5 acres of estuarine waters were located on the islands. Nearly 85,000 acres of these waters were identified in the broader survey area which included seven NWI maps (see Appendix B).

Table 2. Extent of wetlands associated with islands in the Boston Harbor Islands National Recreation Area based on an update of National Wetlands Inventory maps.

Ecological System	Aquatic Habitat	Acreage
Estuarine	Aquatic Bed	33.8
	Emergent Wetland	81.9
	----------------------------------	-------
	Vegetated Wetland	115.7
	Mussel Reef	60.4
	Rocky Shore	48.1
	Unconsolidated Shore	741.6
	----------------------------------	----------
	Nonvegetated Wetland	850.1
	Total Estuarine Wetland	*965.8*
Marine	Aquatic Bed	86.7
	----------------------------------	--------
	Vegetated Wetland	86.7
	Mussel Reef	26.4
	Rocky Shore	35.1
	Unconsolidated Shore	131.0
	----------------------------------	---------
	Nonvegetated Wetland	192.5
	Total Marine Wetland	*279.2*
Palustrine	Emergent Wetland	5.9
	Forested Wetland	1.0
	Scrub-Shrub Wetland	0.8
	----------------------------------	-------
	Vegetated Wetland	7.7
	Unconsolidated Bottom	13.2
	Unconsolidated Shore	9.9
	----------------------------------	-------
	Nonvegetated Wetland	23.1
	Total Palustrine Wetland	*30.8*
All Wetlands		1,275.8

Figure 3. Wetlands classified by Cowardin et al. (1979) (simplified for this figure).

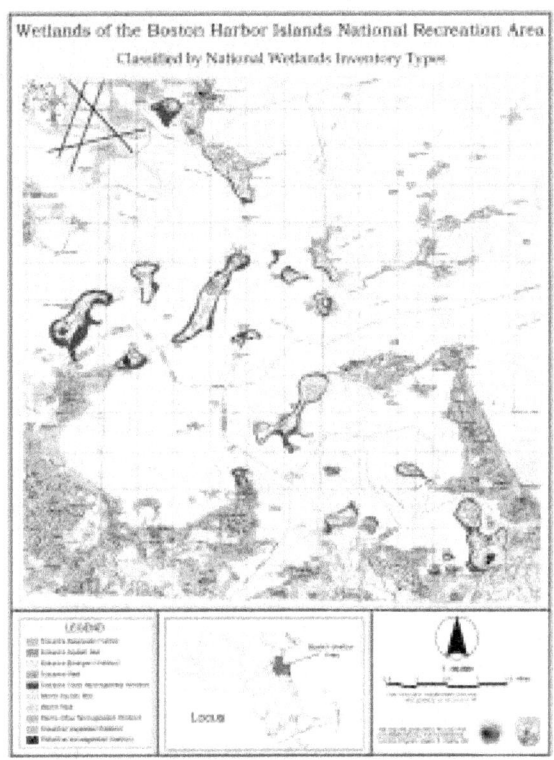

(Click here for image)

Table 3. Wetland acreage summaries by island following Cowardin et al. (1979).

Island	System	Wetland Type	Acreage (total/island)
Bumpkin	Estuarine	Unconsolidated Shore	20.6 (20.6)
Button	Estuarine	Emergent	1.5
		Unconsolidated Shore	4.9 (6.4)
Calf	Estuarine	Emergent	1.6
	Marine	Aquatic Bed	18.3
		Rocky Shore	5.1
		Unconsolidated Shore	2.1 (27.1)
Deer	Estuarine	Unconsolidated Shore	26.8
	Marine	Aquatic Bed	5.6
		Rocky Shore	3.6
		Unconsolidated Shore	47.6 (83.6)
Gallops	Estuarine	Aquatic Bed	1.3
		Rocky Shore	2.1
		Unconsolidated Shore	19.3 (22.7)
Georges	Estuarine	Reef	3.1
		Unconsolidated Shore	8.1
	Marine	Reef	9.5 (20.7)
Grape	Estuarine	Emergent	9.9
		Reef	15.8
		Unconsolidated Shore	22.3 (48.0)
Great Brewster	Marine	Aquatic Bed	5.9
		Rocky Shore	4.6
		Unconsolidated Shore	49.6
	Palustrine	Emergent	0.4 (60.5)
Green	Marine	Aquatic Bed	13.7
		Rocky Shore	2.9 (16.6)
Hangman	Estuarine	Aquatic Bed	2.1
		Emergent	0.4
		Unconsolidated Shore	1.6 (4.1)
Langlee	Estuarine	Rocky Shore	2.2
		Unconsolidated Shore	4.9 (7.1)
Little Brewster	Marine	Reef	7.5
		Rocky Shore	3.0
		Unconsolidated Shore	0.9 (11.4)
Little Calf	Marine	Aquatic Bed	4.7 (4.7)

Table 3 (continued).

Long	Estuarine	Rocky Shore	23.2
		Unconsolidated Shore	88.8
	Palustrine	Emergent	3.0
		Unconsolidated Bottom	0.7
			(115.7)
Lovells	Estuarine	Emergent	1.1
		Reef	20.5
		Unconsolidated Shore	8.7
	Marine	Aquatic Bed	9.4
		Reef	9.4
		Unconsolidated Shore	30.9
	Palustrine	Emergent	0.2
			(80.2)
Middle Brewster	Marine	Aquatic Bed	6.3
		Rocky Shore	7.0
	Palustrine	Emergent	0.1
			(13.4)
Moon	Estuarine	Aquatic Bed	1.6
		Unconsolidated Shore	24.6
	Palustrine	Unconsolidated Shore	9.9
			(36.1)
Nixes Mate	Estuarine	Unconsolidated Shore	11.5
			(11.5)
Nut	Estuarine	Rocky Shore	5.3
		Unconsolidated Shore	13.2
			(18.5)
Outer Brewster	Marine	Aquatic Bed	11.0
		Rocky Shore	8.8
			(19.8)
Peddocks	Estuarine	Emergent	19.1
		Reef	16.3
		Rocky Shore	6.7
		Unconsolidated Shore	75.4
			(117.5)
Raccoon	Estuarine	Aquatic Bed	2.9
		Emergent	2.4
		Unconsolidated Shore	1.2
			(6.5)
Ragged	Estuarine	Aquatic Bed	0.6
		Unconsolidated Shore	7.9
			(8.5)
Rainsford	Estuarine	Aquatic Bed	2.3
		Rocky Shore	4.9
		Unconsolidated Shore	20.5
			(27.7)
Sarah	Estuarine	Aquatic Bed	8.1
			(8.1)
Shag Rocks	Marine	Aquatic Bed	8.2
			(8.2)
Sheep	Estuarine	Aquatic Bed	4.1
		Emergent	1.1
		Unconsolidated Shore	6.7
			(11.9)

Table 3 (continued).

Slate	Estuarine	Aquatic Bed	13.9
		Reef	4.9
		Unconsolidated Shore	6.0
			(24.8)
Snake	Estuarine	Aquatic Bed	5.1
		Emergent	13.4
		Unconsolidated Shore	62.4
			(80.9)
Spectacle	Estuarine	Rocky Shore	0.8
		Unconsolidated Shore	39.8
			(40.6)
The Graves	Marine	Aquatic Bed	3.7
			(3.7)
Thompson	Estuarine	Emergent	19.4
		Rocky Shore	2.9
		Unconsolidated Shore	187.2
	Palustrine	Emergent	1.0
			(210.5)
Worlds End	Estuarine	Emergent	12.2
		Unconsolidated Shore	71.2
	Palustrine	Emergent	1.2
		Forested	1.0
		Scrub-shrub	0.8
		Unconsolidated Bottom	12.5
			(98.9)

Table 4. Wetlands of the Boston Harbor Islands NRA classified by landscape position, landform, and water flow path according to Tiner (2000).

Landscape Position	Landform	Water Flow Path	Acreage
Estuarine	Fringe	Bidirectional-tidal	951.8
	Island	Bidirectional-tidal	12.4
Marine	Fringe	Bidirectional-tidal	266.0
	Island	Bidirectional-tidal	14.9
Terrene	Basin*	Isolated	30.7

----

*Includes 23.0 acres of ponds.

Figure 4. Wetlands classified by landscape position and landform (Tiner 2000).

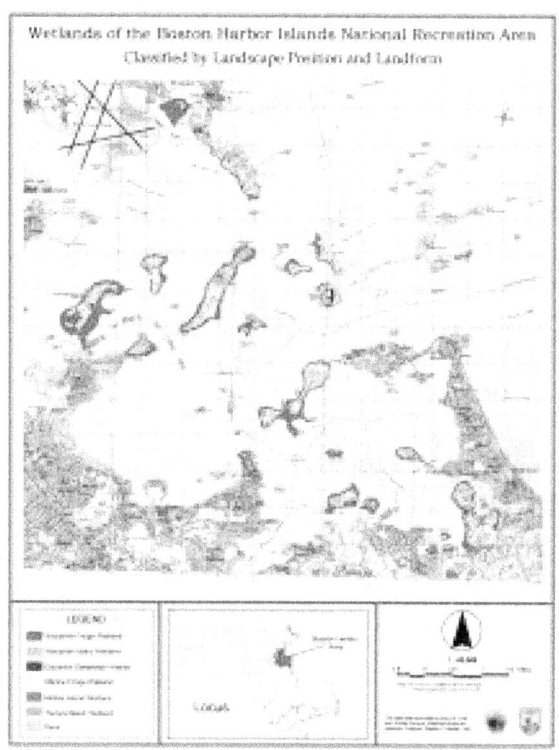

(Click here for image)

Wetland Communities

As mentioned earlier, most of the wetlands are intertidal flats (including narrow beaches) composed of unconsolidated substrates exposed at low and extreme low tide (Figure 5). Mussel reefs dominated by blue mussel (<u>Mytilus</u> <u>edulis</u>) are also prominent in the lower intertidal zone (Figures 6 and 7). Rocky shores may be devoid of vegetation or covered by brown macroalgae (<u>Ascophyllum</u> <u>nodosum</u> and <u>Fucus</u> spp.) (Figure 8).

Most of the vegetated wetlands are estuarine emergent wetlands (Figures 9-13). These wetlands are dominated by halophytes (salt-tolerant plants). Smooth cordgrass (<u>Spartina</u> <u>alterniflora</u>) forms nearly pure stands in the low marsh (the regularly flooded zone - subject to daily tidal inundation). A short form of this species along with other halophytes typify the high marsh (the irregularly flooded zone - flooding less often than daily). The more abundant high marsh species include low-growing plants such as salt hay grass (<u>Spartina</u> <u>patens</u>) and salt grass (<u>Distichlis</u> <u>spicata</u>), while a tall grass, common reed (<u>Phragmites</u> <u>australis</u>) is also common, especially along the upland border and in more brackish conditions. See Tiner (1987) for descriptions and illustrations of tidal wetland flora common to the northeastern United States. One freshwater marsh observed on Thompson Island was dominated by a millet grass (<u>Echinochloa</u> sp.) with several other species present including two invasive plants - purple loosestrife (<u>Lythrum</u> <u>salicaria</u>) and common reed (Figure 14).

Table 5 presents a few examples of Boston Harbor Islands NRA wetland plant communities based on our limited field work. See Bell et al. (2002) for detailed descriptions of intertidal communities and their biota.

Figure 5. Tidal flat and beach (estuarine unconsolidated shore) exposed at low tide on Langlee Island. (photo: ©Sherman Morss, Jr.)

Figure 6. Mussel reef in Boston Harbor. (R. Tiner photo)

Figure 7. Close-up of mussel reef. (R. Tiner photo)

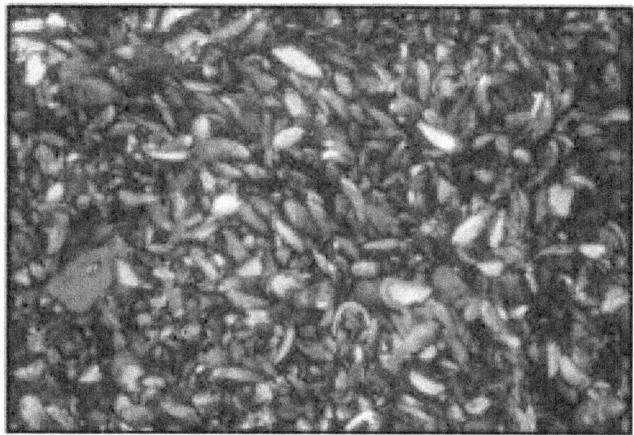

Figure 8. Vegetated rocky shore at Calf Island. (photo: ©Sherman Morss, Jr.)

Figure 9. Salt marsh on Thompson Island. (R. Tiner photo)

Figure 10. Salt marsh on Grape Island with mussel reef in foreground. (R. Tiner photo)

Figure 11. Salt marsh on Peddocks Island. (photo: ©Sherman Morss, Jr.)

Figure 12. Salt marsh on Ragged Island. (photo: ©Sherman Morss, Jr.)

Figure 13. Oligohaline marsh on Grape Island. (R. Tiner photo)

Figure 14. Freshwater marsh (palustrine emergent wetland) on Thompson Island.
(R. Tiner photo)

Table 5. Examples of wetland plant communities in the Boston Harbor Islands NRA.

Wetland Type (Location)	Dominant Species	Associated Species
Estuarine Emergent (Thompson Island)	*Spartina patens- S. alterniflora* (short form)	*Limonium* sp., *Suaeda* sp., *Salicornia* sp., *S. alterniflora* (tall form), *Solidago sempervirens, Atriplex patula*
Estuarine Emergent (Thompson Island)	*S. alterniflora*	*Distichlis spicata, S. patens, P. australis, Salicornia europaea, S. sempervirens, A. patula, Limonium* sp.
Estuarine Emergent (Peddocks Island)	*S. alterniflora*	*D. spicata, P. australis, S. sempervirens, A. patula, Iva frutescens, Limonium* sp., *Typha angustifolia, Juncus gerardii, Scirpus robustus, Calystegia sepium, Scirpus pungens, Puccinellia* sp., *Agropyron repens, S. patens*
Estuarine Emergent (Grape Island)	*S. patens-D. spicata*	(on edge) *P. australis, Epilobium* sp., *Galium* sp., *S. sempervirens, Eupatorium serotinum, Circium canadense, Lythrum salicaria, Agrostis* sp., *Rubus* sp.
Estuarine Emergent Oligohaline (Grape Island)	*P. australis*	*S. pungens, Lythrum salicaria, S. robustus, Verbena hastata, Galium* sp., *S. patens, Scirpus cyperinus, Epilobium* sp., *Agrostis palustris, Onoclea sensibilis, C. canadense* Note: This slightly brackish (oligohaline) wetland is inundated by salt water during overwash events.
Palustrine Emergent Seasonally Flooded (Thompson Island)	*Echinochloa* sp.	*L. salicaria, Eleocharis* sp., *Panicum rigidulum, P. australis, S. robustus, Polygonum pensylvanicum, V. hastata, Erechtites hieracifolia, Cyperus* sp., *C. sepium, T. angustifolia*

Preliminary Assessment of Wetland Functions

Since most of the wetlands are estuarine wetlands, the preliminary assessment of wetland functions is not as interesting as it would be if the wetland diversity was greater. Table 6 summarizes the results by function. Given that the Boston Harbor Islands NRA wetlands are mostly estuarine and marine intertidal marshes, rocky shores, and tidal flats (including intertidal mussel reefs), it is not surprising that most of the wetlands in this area are significant for surface water detention, retention of sediments, coastal storm surge detention and shoreline stabilization, provision of fish and shellfish habitat, and provision of waterfowl and waterbird habitat. Vegetated wetlands represented only a two percent of the wetlands, hence the low percent of wetlands that was identified as significant for nutrient transformation and other wildlife habitat.

Table 6. Wetlands of potential significance for performing various functions in the Boston Harbor Islands NRA. <u>Note</u>: None of the islands had any streams, therefore no wetlands were significant for this streamflow maintenance.

Function	Predicted Level of Significance	Wetland Acres	Percent of Wetland Acreage in BHINRA
Surface Water Detention	High	1,245.1	98%
	Moderate	30.7	2%
Nutrient Transformation	High	210.1	16%
Retention of Sediments	High	881.0	69%
	Moderate	311.6	22%
Coastal Storm Surge Detention/Shoreline Stabilization	High	1,217.8	95%
Provision of Fish and Shellfish Habitat	High	1,245.1	98%
	Moderate	13.2	1%
Provision of Waterfowl and Waterbird Habitat	High	1,075.1	84%
	Moderate	14.4	1%
Provision of Other Wildlife Habitat	High	0	0%
	Moderate	89.6	7%

Summary

A total of 1,276 acres of wetlands were inventoried for the Boston Harbor Islands NRA. These wetlands were dominated by marine and estuarine intertidal types, mostly nonvegetated unconsolidated shores (i.e., tidal flats). Only 82 acres of estuarine vegetated wetlands (i.e., salt/brackish marshes) were inventoried, while 87 acres of intertidal blue mussel reefs were surveyed. Freshwater wetlands were extremely limited on the islands, with only 31 acres mapped. Most of these wetlands were small ponds. The Boston Harbor Islands NRA wetlands were predicted to perform numerous functions, with most of the wetlands designated as potentially significant for surface water detention, sediment retention, coastal storm surge detention and shoreline stabilization, fish and shellfish habitat, and waterfowl and waterbird habitat.

Acknowledgments

Funding for this project was provided by the National Park Service (NPS). Norm Farris served as project officer for the NPS. Ralph Tiner was principal investigator for the U.S. Fish and Wildlife Service (FWS) and was responsible for study design, data analysis, and report preparation. Wetland photointerpretation was performed by John Swords (FWS). The National Wetlands Inventory Center (St. Petersburg, FL) provided quality control of draft inventory products to insure national consistency. Herb Bergquist (FWS) classified wetlands according to hydrogeomorphic properties, performed GIS analyses, generated statistics for tables, and created figures for this report. Charles Roman and Norm Farris (NPS) assisted in field work along with Rick Bell (New England Aquarium) who also provided data from his field investigations of intertidal wetlands. Sherman Morss Jr. gratuitously permitted use of his photographs for this report. Deb DiQuinzio and Mary Raczko (NPS) provided information on official park boundaries and island names.

References

Bell, R. M. Chandler, R. Buchsbaum, and C. Roman. 2002. Boston Harbor Islands Intertidal Biotic Overview and Assessment. National Park Service, Boston, MA.

Cowardin, L.M., V. Carter, F.C. Golet, and E.T. LaRoe. 1979. Classification of Wetlands and Deepwater Habitats of the United States. U.S. Fish and Widlife Service, Washington, DC. FWS/OBS-79/31.

Tiner, R.W. 2000. Keys to Waterbody Type and Hydrogeomorphic-type Wetland Descriptors for U.S. Waters and Wetlands (Operational Draft). U.S. Fish and Wildlife Service, Region 5, Hadley, MA.

Tiner, R.W. 1999. Wetland Indicators: A Guide to Wetland Identification, Delineation, Classification, and Mapping. Lewis Publishers, CRC Press, Boca Raton, FL.

Tiner, R.W. 1990. Use of high-altitude aerial photography for inventorying forested wetlands in the United States. For. Ecol. Manage. 33/34: 593-604.

Tiner, R.W. 1987. A Field Guide to Coastal Wetland Plants of the Northeastern United States. University of Massachusetts Press, Amherst, MA.

Tiner, R., M. Starr, H. Bergquist, and J. Swords. 2000. Watershed-based Wetland Characterization for Maryland's Nanticoke River and Coastal Bays Watersheds: A Preliminary Assessment Report. U.S. Fish and Wildlife Service, National Wetlands Inventory (NWI) Program, Northeast Region, Hadley, MA. NWI technical report (posted on the web at: http://wetlands.fws.gov).

Tiner, R. S. Schaller, D. Petersen, K. Snider, K. Ruhlman, and J. Swords. 1999. Wetland Characterization Study and Preliminary Assessment of Wetland Functions for the Casco Bay Watershed, Southern Maine. U.S. Fish and Wildlife Service, National Wetlands Inventory (NWI) Program, Northeast Region, Hadley, MA. NWI technical report.

Appendices

Appendix A. Legend for wetland and deepwater habitat classification following Cowardin et al. 1979.

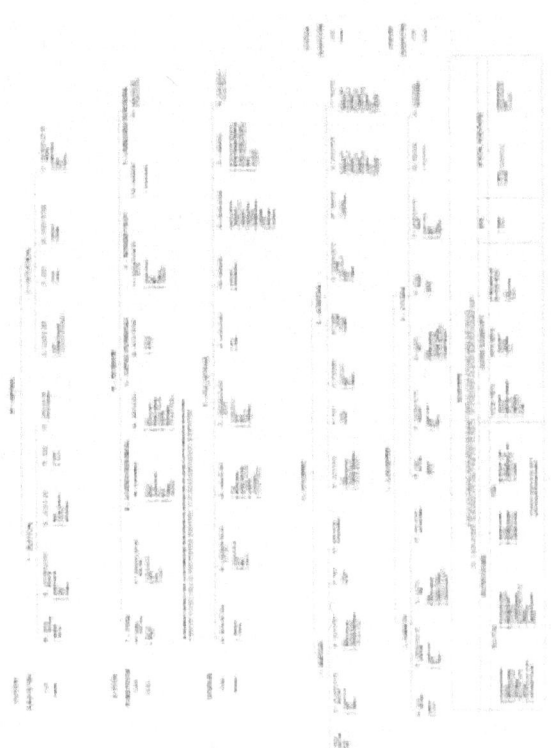

(Click here for image)

Appendix B. Extent of wetlands and deepwater habitats in and around the Boston Harbor Islands NRA based on an update of seven NWI maps in this locale.

Ecological System	Aquatic Habitat	Acreage
Estuarine	Deepwater Habitat	24,771.0
	Aquatic Bed	433.2
	Emergent Wetland	3,868.0
	Mussel Reef	62.2
	Rocky Shore	53.8
	Scrub-Shrub Wetland	6.9
	Unconsolidated Shore	4,656.2
Lacustrine	Deepwater Habitat	2,747.8
	Unconsolidated Shore	0.2
Marine	Aquatic Bed	1,155.0
	Deepwater Habitat	59,852.0
	Mussel Reef	26.4
	Rocky Shore	121.2
	Unconsolidated Shore	1,791.0
Palustrine	Aquatic Bed	0.4
	Emergent Wetland	919.3
	Forested Wetland	8,203.5
	Scrub-Shrub Wetland	1,032.1
	Unconsolidated Bottom	764.0
	Unconsolidated Shore	10.1
Riverine	Perennial Deepwater Habitat	755.4
	Intermittent Streambed	59.9

www.ingramcontent.com/pod-product-compliance
Lightning Source LLC
Chambersburg PA
CBHW080749290526
45790CB00008B/3381